When Your Time Was Right

Books are available in quantity for educational,
business, promotional or premium use.
For information, contact ALIVE Book Publishing at:
alivebookpublishing.com, or call (925) 837-7303.

Book Design by Alex Johnson

ISBN 13: 978-1-63132-162-7

Library of Congress Control Number: 2022905805

Library of Congress Cataloging-in-Publication Data available on request.

Published in the United States of America
by ALIVE Book Publishing
an imprint of Advanced Publishing LLC
3200 A Danville Blvd., Suite 204, Alamo, California 94507
alivebookpublishing.com

Printed in the United States of America

10 9 8 7 6 5 4 3 2 1

When Your Time Was Right

Written by
Valerie Kincaid

Illustrated by
Tori Higa

ABOOKS
Alive Book Publishing

This is for our children.

Elijah, we felt like we waited too long for you.

Lukas, we didn't expect you would come so quickly.

Both of you came in His perfect time,

and we are so grateful for you.

Your dad and I love you so much.

This is also written for all of the couples

that have ever felt the ache of waiting to start a family.

Your daddy and I had so much love for each other, it overflowed.

We decided we needed you to pour all that extra love into.

We decided it was time to try to start our family.

We couldn't wait to meet you!

We thought you would
come real soon.

But God knew that
it just wasn't
the RIGHT time yet.

We waited for you..

and waited.. and waited.

We were so sad and thought
that you might never come.

We were giving up hope.

We wanted you more than anything right then

but we had to learn to be patient,
to trust God,
and to be grateful for each moment.

And when His time was perfect,
God sent you to us.

Even though we had to wait a long time,
we knew the moment we met you

that you came just when you were meant to.

Time had made us
into who we were supposed to be to raise you.

And every day that passes, we thank God for you, our little love.
His timing was perfect.

About the Author

Valerie Kincaid is a California native who calls the Bay Area home. Her hobbies include working out, spending time in nature, and reading. She has a passion for child development and working with children. She helped launch *Our City Center* in Berkeley in 2020 as Children's Ministry Coordinator. Her happy place is anywhere in nature with her amazing husband, Brandon, and their beloved children, Elijah and Lukas.

About the Illustrator

Tori Higa is inspired by her faith, family, friends, coffee shops, people watching, and anything vintage. She has always loved making art and considers it a high honor to make books for kids to inspire them in the ways of the Lord. She currently lives in Southern California with her husband, Branden, two kids, Kai and Maile, and a playful dog named Edie.

ABOOKS

ALIVE Books, ALIVE Book Publishing and ALIVE Publishing Group are imprints of
Advanced Publishing LLC,
3200 A Danville Blvd., Suite 204, Alamo, California 94507

Telephone: 925.837.7303
alivebookpublishing.com

CPSIA information can be obtained
at www.ICGtesting.com
Printed in the USA
LVHW070731270522
719903LV00006B/66

9 781631 321627